Y0-CDJ-704

CONTEND
FOR THE FAITH

Sermons by
Dr. Tom Neal
and
Dr. Jack Hyles

Berean Publications
4459 US Highway 17
Fleming Island, Florida 32003
A Ministry of Berean Baptist Church

Copyright © 2009 by Berean Publications

All rights reserved. No part of this book may be reproduced or transmitted in any form or by any means without permission in writing from the publisher.

Published in Fleming Island, Florida, by Berean Publications

The following written material was originally preached in the pulpit of Berean Baptist Church and later edited by Berean Publications.

All Scriptures quoted in this text are from the King James Bible.

ISBN 978-0-9771829-2-3

Printed and bound in the United States of America

II Timothy 4:7
I have fought a good fight, I have finished my course, I have kept the faith:

Dedication

This book is dedicated to all of the brave men and women throughout history who have paid the ultimate price for their stand for the faith.

> *...and others were tortured, not accepting deliverance; that they might obtain a better resurrection: And others had trial of cruel mockings and scourgings, yea, moreover of bonds and imprisonment: They were stoned, they were sawn asunder, were tempted, were slain with the sword: they wandered about in sheepskins and goatskins; being destitute, afflicted, tormented; (Of whom the world was not worthy:) they wandered in deserts, and in mountains, and in dens and caves of the earth.*

Hebrews 11:35-38

Foreword
by Dr. Greg Neal

I have had the wonderful privilege of being reared in a preacher's home. I have been exposed to preachers and preaching my entire life. I was shown by example that being a preacher was not a profession but a calling. I have been shown that being a man of God is a way of life and not a title. I have been shown that being a preacher is not about belonging to an exclusive fraternity but it signifies a unique relationship. When I felt the call to preach as a child, I knew what kind of preacher I wanted to be.

In my lifetime I have heard the two men whose sermons are in this book more than any other preachers. Upon my college graduation and entry into the ministry, I wanted to be a preacher that had the courage to say what needed to be said no matter what the cost. I also wanted to be the kind of preacher that had the life and Holy Spirit power to back up what was said from the pulpit. I wanted to be a preacher that contended for the Faith.

As I pen these words, much has changed since my call to preach and my graduation from Bible College. Dr. Hyles is now in Heaven, and I now serve as my father's co-pastor. One thing, however, has not changed. I still want to be a preacher like Tom Neal and Jack Hyles. There are no two men in my lifetime that have been better examples of preachers who were faithful to contend for the faith. It is my belief that through these two sermons you will see the scriptural command to contend for the faith and receive inspiration to likewise do so. May God bless you and I as we are faithful to do our part in defending the faith.

May our testimony be as the Apostle Paul's when we come to the end of our life. *I have fought a good fight, I have finished my course, I have kept the faith.* II Timothy 4:7

Table of Contents

Biography of Dr. Tom Neal

Dr. Tom Neal surrendered to preach when he was nineteen years of age. After he surrendered to preach in Atlanta, Georgia, he enrolled in Tennessee Temple College in Chattanooga, Tennessee. In the fall of 1966, he started his training under Dr. Lee Roberson's ministry at Highland Park Baptist Church.

While attending Tennessee Temple College, he earned a Graduate of Theology Degree in August of 1969 and a Bachelor of Bible Degree in August of 1971. Upon graduation, he served as an Associate Pastor of Mt. Vernon Baptist Church in Stockbridge, Georgia for three years. Then the Lord led him to Lake Butler, Florida, serving the Trinity Baptist Church for three years as the pastor. With a heart for pastors and a heart for people, God used Dr. Neal in full-time evangelism for the next three and a half years.

It was in November of 1980 that the Lord led Dr. Tom Neal to Orange Park, Florida, to his present pastorate at Berean Baptist Church. He has led Berean Baptist Church from a handful of people to a thriving ministry in one of the fastest growing areas of northeast Florida. He has been honored with Doctorate Degrees from Heritage Baptist University in Indianapolis, Indiana; Trinity Baptist College in Jacksonville, Florida; Hyles-Anderson College in Crown Point, Indiana; and Baptist College of America in Kokomo, Indiana. In the fall of 1998, he started Berean Baptist College to train future servants of God for the work of God around the world.

His goals and desire are to do all he can to encourage others to contend for the faith and to use his life for the propagation of the Gospel around the world.

CONTEND FOR THE FAITH

In verse 3, the Bible says, *that ye should earnestly contend for the faith...* Earnestly means with some effort or working with diligence. In the context of this little book, Jude is speaking to you, to me, and to every Christian. He is speaking to those who have experienced the common salvation. He is not saying that salvation is just a common thing, but he is saying that everybody that has ever been saved has been saved the same way. It ought to stir you to think that when Peter said *like precious faith*, he was talking about the faith you and I have. Hence, Jude says to those who have been saved, you are supposed to be contending for the faith. You should not just contend, but *earnestly contend for the faith*. Contending should be a priority at the top of the list. I am afraid that many people do not understand what the Bible is saying when it says *contend for the faith*.

If the Bible tells us that we ought to do something earnestly, we should find out what God expects from us. As I began to study what the word *contend* means, it became a word that I love. I realized the word *contend* means "to strive, to judge, or to enter into judgment." People should strive and learn to judge regarding the faith. I am told by God to enter into judgment about the faith and to judge differently. We are to judge our faith differently than we would judge the color of a carpet, the color of a building, or anything else that really does not amount to anything with eternal value. I discovered that this is the same word that is used in Nehemiah Chapter 13. Nehemiah said, "I contended with them and cursed them." I have never cursed people publicly, but I have contended for issues of the faith. God wants us to *earnestly contend for the faith*. Contending is not only my responsibility but also the responsibility of everyone who is saved. Every preacher, layman, soulwinner, and child of God is responsible to earnestly contend for the faith. I want to give you an outline of the book of Jude to help you understand what is meant by *contend for the faith*.

Dr. Tom Neal

CONTEND FOR PURE DOCTRINES

In verses 1-10, Jude teaches us to *contend for the faith*. He is saying that we ought to contend for that great body of faith that has been preserved and handed down by our forefathers to you and me. Therefore, we are to contend, to get angry, and to judge some things differently when someone tries to change and pervert that great historic body of faith. What am I talking about? I am talking about salvation by grace through faith–simple salvation. I still believe you are saved by grace through faith. I still believe that you are saved by simply trusting Jesus Christ, and that is all it takes. Therefore, when somebody says that there is another way to Heaven or tries to add to salvation, I am supposed to fret myself. I am supposed to judge differently and be upset with him. I am supposed to get ready to have a contentious spirit or a bad spirit about any person who would pervert the doctrine of salvation. I am talking about the blood of Jesus Christ that is still alive today. The blood is in Heaven, and it testifies of our salvation. The blood did not disappear into the ground at Calvary. I am supposed to be upset when a man contradicts that. I am supposed to be irate when someone makes light of the blood of the Lord Jesus Christ.

When Jesus died on the cross, He died in my place. He died and took my punishment for me. It should have been me who paid for my sins and who suffered as Jesus suffered on the cross of Calvary. When somebody says his vicarious suffering was not so, I should be disturbed enough to want to do something about it. Positionally, as far as God is concerned, I died at Calvary with Jesus and was resurrected with Him. That is the way God sees me, and I should be angry if somebody tries to take that away from me.

When someone would question the birth of our Saviour or the doctrine of Heaven, I am to fret myself. We know there is a place called Heaven that is a resting place for the saints of God. Heaven is a place where God lives and where the blood of Christ is on the mercy seat. Heaven is a place where the angels rejoice and praise the Savior forever, and I shall go to that place one day. I am supposed to be upset when someone tries to tell me there is no such place.

When someone tries to tell me that Hell is not real or that men and women do not die and go to Hell and burn forever, I am supposed to keep believing that Hell is a real place. When a man comes along and says there is no place like Hell, I am supposed to be upset. Hell is a real place where the screams of the damned are heard.

I do not believe in the universal church or the invisible church. I believe in the doctrine of the local church. We should not fall prey to the ideas that have been propagated by the universal church or by the electronic church. Neither of these institutions are churches. There is only one church, the local New Testament church. I ought to fret myself about that doctrine.

I ought to fret myself about the Word of God. I still believe we have a Bible, the King James Bible. God has preserved His Word. I do not care what the college professors say or how much they make fun of us fundamentalists! I am going to get a contentious spirit when somebody questions the Bible. I am going to question the man's motives, his beliefs, and his purpose if he be not true to the precious Word of God. I am saying that it is time for Bible-believing fundamentalists to once again start contending for the faith. I am talking about Oliver Greene's fundamentalism. I am talking about Lester Roloff's fundamentalism, John Rice's fundamentalism, and Jack Hyles's fundamentalism. It is time we get a contentious spirit about fundamentalism. It is time we say, "I am going to contend for the faith." All of us are responsible to contend for the faith.

Dr. Tom Neal

CONTEND AGAINST FALSE TEACHERS

In verses 11-19, there is a second meaning for *contend for the faith*. We are to contend against the false teachers. It is permissible to have a bad spirit toward John McArthur! It is all right to get angry with false prophets and teachers. I am to contend against false teachers. It is time we take off the white gloves. People may say, "Well, let's disagree, but don't be disagreeable." How do you do that? How do you disagree with somebody and not be disagreeable? It is time we decide to become angry with people who try to change the body of faith that has been entrusted to us by our forefathers. A fellow once said to me, "You have a bad spirit." That is correct! I am glad that he understands where I am coming from when it comes to faith and beliefs. I am going to have a bad spirit against certain people. I hear people say, "Oh, now they are good men." I am so tired of hearing that. If a man teaches false doctrine, am I supposed to say that he is a good man? That is not what Jude said. Jude likened these false teachers to brute beasts, and ungodly, lascivious men. He compares them to fornicators in verse 7. He said they are filthy dreamers that speak evil of authority. Despising authority, these false teachers are spots in your feasts of charity and are clouds without water. Jude says these men are trees whose fruit withereth and are as raging waves and wandering stars. They are murmurers and complainers that are void of the spirit. This is what God says about these false teachers. It does not sound as if God thinks that these are good men.

When you go home on Sunday night and turn on Charles Stanley or Joel Osteen, you are not listening to a good man. These are men who have propagated false doctrine. You are not listening to a good man if he perverts the Word of God. I am tired of Baptist people listening to such men. It would be better for you to watch something else secular than to watch men like these. Some people say, "Well, John McArthur is a good man." He is not a good man. Chuck Swindoll is not a good man. These perverters of the faith are not good men; they are evil men. The Bible says I ought to have a contentious and angry spirit toward them. I have made up my mind that I do not like these men, and I am never going to like them.

You may say, "You are supposed to like everybody." No, you are not supposed to like everybody. There are certain people and things that I have on a list that I will never like. You have to decide not to like some things, or you are going to change or compromise. I am not going to meet with the ministerial association and try to be like those men. I want to sabotage their work. I do not want to try to help somebody who is a perverter of the Truth, but rather stop them. I am tired of God's people saying, "Oh, they are good men!" No, they are not good men. I will tell you who are the good men. Lee Roberson, J. Frank Norris, Oliver B. Greene, Tom Malone, Jack Hyles, Harold Sightler —these were good men among many others.

We have good men, and they are the ones who are being cursed. It is time that those of us who know the truth expose those who want to destroy the Truth and our faith. They want to take away from us what has been entrusted to us by our past heroes of the faith. Why should our forefathers have to do all of the contending and fighting while we do nothing? The hour is come. It is time that you start fighting and start contending. We contend for the faith when we get rid of Swindoll, Stanley, Dobson, Osteen, and Rick Warren. You might say, "You have a bad spirit." You are right! It is time that we *contend for the faith*. It is time that we contend against the false teachers.

Dr. Tom Neal

CONTEND WITH THE FAITH

There is a third meaning in verses 20-25. Here Jude tells us to *contend with the faith*. Does it matter who has the right Bible if we do not take that Bible and keep somebody out of Hell? What does it matter if we believe right about the church, the blood, and the plan of salvation if we do not use it to get people saved? I am supposed to fight against false doctrine and false teachers.

There are some men who love the faith, but that is where they stop. I have news for you. If you do not go on and do what the rest of this Book says and *contend with the faith*, you are useless. You are not helping or doing anything to stem the tide of what is going on in our country today. We must have people who say, "Bless God, I will not be moved in what I believe. I'll stand against those who try to pervert what I believe. I'll take the Truth that I have, and I will spread the Truth everywhere that I can." It is senseless to believe right if we do not do right. Doing right is *contending with the faith*.

In verses 22-25, Jude tells us that there are three ways to *contend with the faith*. Verse 22 states, *And of some have compassion, making a difference.* There are some of you who were saved because somebody had compassion. Somebody wept over you and begged God for you. Somebody stood before you with tears streaming down his cheeks and begged you to be saved. It was the compassion of somebody with the Truth that brought you to Christ; hence, you were saved and transformed by the grace of God. Oh, how we need a rebirth of compassion. Jude says we are to *contend with the faith* by having compassion toward lost people. Compassion means that we need to have some prayer meetings about lost people and that we need to earnestly tell the world about Christ. There are some people who can only be won to Christ with compassion.

CONTEND FOR THE FAITH

Then Jude tells us something else in verse 23: *And others save with fear.* Do you know what that means? There are some of you who were saved out of fear. Somebody scared you to death with Hell. Somebody dangled your feet out over Hell, and you felt your hair singe. You smelled the smoke of the eternal flames. You were scared; hence, you cried out to God for mercy, and you were saved. Contending with the faith is knocking on a door and telling somebody that he is going to Hell if he does not get saved. It is not just enough to contend for the faith by calling Joel Osteen's name. You must contend with the faith. You must take the faith and lead others to Christ with compassion and with fear. You must confront them. That is confrontational, "in-your-face" soulwinning.

The third way to *contend with the faith* is found in the latter part of verse 23, *pulling them out of the fire.* This means that we will stand before lost people that are on their way to Hell, and we must do all that we can do to keep them from going to Hell. We must tell them, "You can't go to Hell. I must stop you. Here is the Truth." That is what pulling them out of the fire means.

This means that we should use methods that the world calls unconventional. Perhaps you may use buses or put on a carnival. Maybe you might give out some hot dogs and hamburgers or give away prizes. You might have a Sunday School campaign. You must stand in front of sinners and say, "Do not go to Hell!" That is what it is all about. You need to get out of your study, and quit your disertational writing and criticizing. Get on a bus route and keep somebody out of Hell. Become a Sunday School teacher, and tell boys and girls about Jesus. Go to a nursing home, and tell an elderly man or woman about Heaven. Only then can you really be a *contender with the faith.*

Jude said there are some people you might save with compassion: you love them; you pray for them; you weep for them. There are some people you might save with fear. Then, there are some you have to snatch out of Hell. The truth is that there are some that will come to church because of a Sunday School promotion and get saved. You might say, "I am going to go to church so that they will leave me alone." That is why some of you went to church. That is what *contending with the faith* will do for you. It is time to *contend with the faith.*

I hear people say, "Preacher, there is no need for an outreach ministry in our area." I then would ask, "Does anybody live in your area?" They will say, "Well, it is all rich folks." So! We do not bring in thousands; but they will hear the Gospel. As Christians, we are supposed to witness to everybody. The Bible says, Christians, I am writing to you. You must earnestly contend, and quit playing. You must apply some energy and strength. Make it your priority to *contend with the faith. Contending with the faith* means that you are going to stand for what is right about the doctrines with which you have been entrusted—the doctrines that have been handed down from Christ Himself. Then, you are going to oppose those who try to change those doctrines. The Bible says to take those doctrines, the doctrine of salvation and the truth of the Gospel, and go contend with that faith.

CONTEND FOR THE FAITH

Jude said in verse 4, *For there are certain men crept in unawares...* These men creep in to do what? They keep us from contending for the faith. Do not judge me harshly because I have called some names and said some pointed things. God told us that men would creep in unawares. They seem just like us. They act as we act. They say they believe what we believe. They look like we look, but they have crept in to keep us from contending for the faith.

CONTEND FOR THE FAITH

Jude said there are *certain men*. Now, who are these *certain men*? In verse 11, we find out who they are. *Woe unto them for they have gone in the way of Cain*. Cain is the first culprit. What did Cain do? He rebelled and attacked the plan of salvation. He tried to change blood redemption and make salvation by works.

I never dreamed that I would live in a day where Baptist people, (independent, fundamental Baptists) do not even understand the plan of salvation. Salvation is the same as it has always been. Lordship salvation asks, "Did you make Jesus Lord?" No, and you did not either. "Have you repented of all of your sins?" No, and you have not either. Salvation is still by *grace through faith*. Salvation is still as simple as bowing your head and asking Jesus to save you. By faith, He will save you. Critics will say, "Well, I just don't believe people get saved in twenty to thirty minutes at a door or on the street or somewhere else." Sometimes they say, "Those kids didn't mean it." We have such questions being propagated by men who have *crept in unawares* and who stand in pulpits and pretend to be what we are. We hear questions like this all the time. "How many of them really meant it? How many of them were sincere? How many of them really, really meant it? How many of them cried? Were they there tithing the next week?" We listen to these questions and say, "Well, that Brother is just..." No, I have news for you, that is not an attack on soulwinners. It is not an attack on those who have been soulwinning. It is an attack on God's plan of salvation. If you believe that you can be saved by any other way than simple faith and trusting in Jesus Christ and His finished work on the cross of Calvary, pray tell, what is the difference between that and believing that you can lose your salvation? What is the difference in that and believing that you are saved by works? It is time we say that it is not an attack on soulwinning, but an attack on God's plan of salvation. It is an attack on how God said man can be saved: God is the One Who chooses how men are to be saved.

These men who creep in and who rebel at the plan of salvation are attacking soulwinning ministries and the bus ministries. You know why they are confused about salvation? They do not talk about their salvation enough. If you tell your testimony repeatedly, it will soon be set. You will not doubt your salvation if you are talking about it. If you go around telling everybody how to be saved or how you were saved, you will not be confused about it. We have doubts about salvation because we are not doing what we are supposed to do—*contend for the faith*. You may say, "I am contending for the faith!" If you are contending then you must tell somebody about Jesus and keep them from going to Hell. You need to go soulwinning in order to *contend for the faith*.

Notice something else that these men do. In verse 11 these men have *gone in the way of Cain, and ran greedily after the error of Balaam for reward*. These men that come in unawares, go *after the error of Balaam*. What did Balaam do? Balaam rebelled at separation. He was a preacher who was not separated. He would not just come out and say, "No, I'm not one of them." He would not curse them as he was asked to do. Instead, he decided to build a bridge. He decided that he was going to mix God's people with the heathen people. Balaam had a price. You know what grieves me? These guys who start in our crowd (the independent, fundamental, Bible-believing, Baptist, soulwinning, separated crowd) gaining our people's love and admiration, and getting our people's money, get a little too big for that belief. They move on to other places, growing their crowd a little bigger and allowing their circle and sphere of influence to reach out into new areas. This is the same thing that Balaam did. God's people ought to be separated people. We ought to be separated not only in the way we look and act but also in doctrine, as well. I believe we are supposed to be separated from those who are not keeping people out of Hell and from those who are trying to make people believe that a "feel good" religion is all you need in this world today. It is time that you and I *contend for the faith.*

There is a crowd today that is trying to get us to join with the Southern Baptists. I am an old-fashioned, independent Baptist; and I have news for you, they "ain't" going to get us to do it. I promise you that they are not. They are having these bridge building conferences. Well, I guarantee you that I am trying to find every bridge they build and destroy it. We are not going to build the bridge back. My children are not going to go to a Southern Baptist church. Our church is not going to the Southern Baptists. We are free and have been liberated. We have the Truth. Why, in God's name do we want to go back to that mess? It is time that we are separated. Nobody preaches in my pulpit that preaches with Southern Baptists. Nobody! If you hear somebody preach for me, and you know that they preach with Southern Baptists, let me know. You might say, "Well, I think that we shouldn't split hairs." No, it is not time to split hairs. It is time to start yanking some hairs. We have a faith for which to contend. We have an old-time fundamentalism that I want my children, my grandchildren, and others to have. Somebody needs to get a contentious, bad spirit about those who are trying to change what we believe.

You may say, "You don't have love." I will guarantee you that I love sinners more than you do. You can go to every church in my town and ask them about me. I will lose every election that you want to have. However, people that we reach out to will say they love me and would fight for me because they know I care. If you have love, you must *contend for the faith.* You must tell the plan of salvation. That crowd that wants us all to join together again are the ones going around saying, "Would you repent of all your sins?" Then, they live as they want all week long. These men rebelled against the plan of salvation and against separation. It is time to *contend for the faith.*

In verse 11 Jude continues, *...and perished in the gainsaying of Core.* What did Core do? He rebelled against authority. Good people do not rebel against authority or try to get you to rebel against authority. If somebody comes to your church to rebel against your pastor, confront them. Do not wait for your preacher to have to preach him out, pray him out, or kick him out. You get rid of him. Good people are not those who rebel against authority or who question soulwinning. Good people are not those who question what you are doing to keep people out of Hell and to build a church. That is not what good people do!

These people rebelled against authority and against the King James Bible. That is what we have today. That is why I think we ought to make more out of the Bible. You see, one of the biggest criticisms that fundamentalist may get is that we believe in the King James Bible. Every time critics say something about that, I yell louder. You should yell louder too. Proclaim that you believe the King James Bible! Why? The reason is that there are people in their churches who are beginning to figure out why one preacher has a Bible and why their preacher does not know where one is. They look at the old-fashioned preacher, and they say, "He knows what he believes. I don't know why he believes it, but I know he has something that he can stand on, and he knows what he believes."

We had a battle not long ago with First Baptist Church of Jacksonville. First Baptist Church had a Rabbi and an Episcopal Priest speak at their service. Remember, this is supposed to be a conservative, Southern Baptist church. They had two charismatic speakers speak also. Well, I decided to put an ad in the newspaper questioning whether they were really Baptists. I said I was going to preach on that subject Sunday night. The press came, and a crowd came with the press. One man became so angry that night that he walked out and slammed the door. He did not even make it through the introduction of the sermon. Later that week, he wrote me a nasty letter full of criticism. A few weeks went by when my secretary came to my door. She was nervous. She said that there was a man here to see me. She handed me his card, and I saw that he was a businessman. She said that he was the one who had written me the letter and that he wanted to see me. She said that he would understand if I did not want to see him, but he would like to see me. I invited him back to my office. He came and sat down. He could hardly look at me. He said, "I hope you didn't read that letter." I told him that I did. He said, "I want to apologize for it. I should never have written it. I don't agree with you. I don't even like you, but I have to apologize to you. I have gone around this town and and have realized that this church has something that no other church has. I don't know how you get it. I don't know why all these poor people out here love you and love this place like they do. I don't know why, but I know one thing. God has showed me that this is His church." He continued, "I could never be apart of it. I probably won't ever like you, but I want you to know that I'm sorry." I told him that I would accept his apology. I would rather have his apology than for me to compromise and have everybody like me.

Jude tells us to *contend for the faith*. That is a big job. Did you know that in contending for the faith, you may get weary? Did you know that you may get discouraged? If you are not careful, you can get a bad spirit. It is all right to have a bad spirit with the false prophets, but we should not have a bad spirit with each other. We should not have a bad spirit about life. We ought to be the happiest and most joyful people. Did you know that Jude tells you how to stay happy while you are contending for the faith?

How do we keep ourselves right? Jude says in verse 20, *But ye, beloved, building up yourselves on your most holy faith...* What does that mean? It means that we do not have to look for something new. What we received when we got saved was all that we needed. We are to build everything for the future on what happened when we were saved. That is the foundation. Who is supposed to build my faith? I am supposed to build my faith. You may say, "Well, the preacher is not building me up." He is not supposed to build you up. You are responsible to build yourself up. The Bible says, *on your most holy faith, praying in the Holy Ghost.* That means you have to encourage yourself. Notice this verse says, *Keep yourselves in the love of God, looking for the mercy of our Lord Jesus Christ unto eternal life.* I am to keep myself in the love of God. How do you keep yourself in the love of God? How do you keep a loving spirit? How do you keep loving people? How do you keep caring about people? How do you avoid getting cynical? Verse 22 says, *And of some have compassion, making a difference.* That is how you keep yourself in love with God. You must keep after sinners. You must have a broken heart and compassion for sinners. That means you must keep doing confrontational soulwinning ... *and pulling them out of the fire.* That means you need to keep on running your buses and keep snatching them out of Hell when they did not plan to be saved. You must keep on having spring and fall programs and special promotions to get people saved. If you keep on doing that, you will keep yourself in the love of God and will keep yourself right. You will be obeying what we all must obey because we are all exhorted to *earnestly contend for the faith.*

CONTEND FOR THE FAITH

Biography of
Dr. Jack Hyles

Jack Hyles began preaching at the age of 19 and has pastored for over half a century. These pastorates include churches that varied in membership from 44 to over 100,000. All of these pastorates, other than one, were in the state of Texas: First, the Marris Chapel Baptist Church of Bogata, Texas; then to the Grange Hall Baptist Church in Marshall, Texas; from there to the Southside Baptist Church of Henderson, Texas; and then to the Miller Road Baptist Church of Garland, Texas. He pastored the Miller Road Baptist Church for over 7 years and saw this church, under the Lord, grow from a membership of 44 to over 4,000. It was from the Miller Road Baptist Church that he was called to his last pastorate at the First Baptist Church in Hammond, Indiana.

Dr. Hyles pastored the First Baptist Church from August, 1959 until his death on February 6, 2001. Under his leadership he was acclaimed to have the "World's Largest Sunday School." During Dr. Hyles' ministry, the First Baptist Church increased in property evaluation to over $30,000,000.

Besides his position as Pastor, Dr. Hyles was the founder of Hyles-Anderson Schools. Dr. Hyles has also served as president of the Baptist Bible College in Denver, Colorado.

Dr. Hyles is the author of over 40 books and pamplets, exceeding over 10 million copies in sales. Dr. Hyles' experience covers numerous evangelistic campaigns, Bible conferences, etc. He has preached in virtually every state in the Union and in many foreign countries.

CONTEND FOR THE FAITH

CONTENDING FOR THE FAITH

Dr. Jack Hyles

I am going to analyze Tom Neal. I am going to tell you exactly why we are as we are. Before we start, I want to tell you that I love you. You had better write that down and look at it every once in a while as I am preaching. I feel as if I am taking coals to Newcastle because Dr. Neal has a better sermon than I have on this text, but I am going to preach this sermon around the country if it hair lips every dog in the country. It needs to be preached, and I think that I am the fellow who needs to preach it. As I said before, Dr. Neal has a sermon on this text that is far better than mine; but I want to underline what he says. I want people to know that I believe what he believes.

In II Timothy 4:7, Paul is ending his life, and he says, *I have fought a good fight, I have finished my course, I have kept the faith.* Now ladies and gentlemen, these are not three things.

CONTEND FOR THE FAITH

This is one thing that is described in three different ways. He said I have fought a good fight; and by the way, I have finished the course. You cannot finish the course without fighting a good fight. "I have kept the faith." You cannot keep the faith without finishing the course. You cannot fight the good fight without keeping the faith. You cannot keep the faith without fighting the good fight. All three of these statements are synonymous. *I have fought a good fight, I have finished my course, I have kept the faith.* Jude 3 says, *Beloved, when I gave all diligence to write unto you of the common salvation, it was needful for me to write unto you, and exhort you that ye should earnestly contend...* That word "contend" means to wrestle, strive, fight, hold fast, guard, combat, war, and so forth. *Ye should earnestly contend for the faith which was once delivered unto the saints.*

FIGHT THE GOOD FIGHT

We are told to *fight the good fight* in I Timothy 6:12. The Apostle Paul said in II Timothy 4:7, *I have fought a good fight.* In II Timothy 2:3, he says, *Endure hardness as a good soldier.* In verse 4, he talks about *no man that warreth entangleth himself.* It sounds to me that we are supposed to fight. David listed his mighty men, and his mighty men were all fighters. One took a spear and killed eight hundred of the enemy. Another killed three hundred in battle. Another slew two lion-like men and one, the Bible says, *hand clave to the sword.* At least eight of the great heroes in Hebrews Chapter 11 were warriors. In verse 34, you will find the phrase *waxed valiant in fight.* In Judges, at least seven of the judges were famous for their warfare: Gideon and his three hundred, Shamgar and his oxgoad, Ehud and his battalion of seven hundred southpaw (left-handed) men, Jephthah and the army that he commanded, Deborah and Barak in the famous war they fought; Othniel who the Bible says that *the Spirit of the Lord came upon him, ...and he went out to war,* and Samson who slew one hundred Philistines with the jawbone of an ass. In Genesis, Abraham went to war to deliver Lot. In Exodus, the armies of Egypt were drowned in the Red Sea. In Deuteronomy 1:41, we read, *...we will go up and fight.* The book of Joshua begins with the battle of Jericho. In Judges, as I already mentioned, at least seven of the judges were warriors and fighters. In I Samuel 4:9 it says, *...quit yourselves like men, and fight.* I am a little tired of these "sissy britches" preachers criticizing men who obey the command of God. As the song says,

Rouse, then, soldiers, rally round the banner,
Ready, steady, pass the word along;
Onward, forward, shout aloud Hosanna!
Christ is Captain of the mighty throng.

II Samuel 22:35 says, *He teacheth my hands to war.* I Kings 22:4 states, *...wilt thou go with me to battle.* II Kings 3:7 speaks of *...wilt thou go with me... to battle?* In I Chronicles 12:8 it says, *...men of war fit for the battle.* In II Chronicles 20:15 it says, *...the battle is not yours, but God's.* In Job 15:24, the Bible says, *...as a king ready to the battle.* Nehemiah 4:17 speaks about those building the wall, *...with one of his hands wrought in the work, and with the other hand held a weapon.* In Ezra 8:22, *...require of the king a band of soldiers.* Psalm 18:34 says, *He teacheth my hands to war...* In Proverbs 20:18 it says, *With good advice make war.* Ecclesiastes 3:8 states, *...a time of war.* In Ecclesiastes 8:8 we read, *...there is no discharge in that war.* In Isaiah 13:5, it speaks about *...weapons of his indignation.* In Jeremiah 48:14, the Bible says, *We are mighty and strong men for the war.* In Daniel Chapter 2, it talks about the stone cut out without hands that will

CONTEND FOR THE FAITH

break in pieces the kingdoms of this world and will establish a kingdom where Christ shall rule and reign for a thousand years. In Joel 3:9 it says, ...*Prepare war.* In Amos 1:14, it talks about *shouting in the day of battle.* Nahum 3:3 talks about lifting up the sword and the spear. Zechariah 10:5 says, ...*and they shall fight, because the Lord is with them.* The Bible does not say that they shall give devotionals because the Lord is with them. It did not say that they would have four o'clock vespers on Sunday afternoon because the Lord is with them. It did not say they will quote poetry because the Lord is with them. It says, *they shall fight, because the Lord is with them.*

In Matthew 8:9, it says, ...*having soldiers unto me.* Luke 14:31 talks about a ...*king going to make war.* In Acts, it talks about Cornelius the Centurion. In Romans 8:37 it says, ...*we are more than conquerors through him that loved us.* In I Corinthians 14:8, ...*who shall prepare himself to the battle.* In II Corinthians 10:4, it talks about the weapons of our warfare. In Ephesians 6:11, it says, *Put on the whole armour of God.* In Ephesians 6:17, it talks about the *sword of the Spirit.* In I Timothy 6:12, *Fight the good fight of faith.* I Timothy 1:18 states, ...*war a good warfare.* Hey! Are you compromisers getting under conviction? Are you little back-scratching, ear-tickling, penny-pinching, nickel-nipping, soft-soaping, tea-and-lemonade compromisers getting under conviction? Are those of you whose Bible study is reading the daily devotional book every morning with half of a verse and a poem and some little sickly, puny, putrid words by some little devotional-type Christian getting under conviction? The Bible talks about the war that is going on. In II Timothy 2:3, we read ...*endure hardness, as a good soldier.* In II Timothy 4:7, *we are told I have fought a good fight.* In Hebrews 11:34, it says they *waxed valiant in fight.* In Jude 3, we are commanded

...earnestly contend for the faith. Revelation 19:11 says, *...and in righteousness he doth judge and make war.*

Now you listen to me! You like us or you do not. You may criticize us all you want; but, Brethren, God's men are fighting men. God's people are fighting people. You cannot be a fundamentalist without fighting. That is one of the qualifications of being a fundamentalist. You have got to fight. Do we sing, "Onward Christian devotionalizers, crawling as to vesper"? No, we sing, "Onward Christian soldiers, marching as to war." Do we sing, "The vesper is on oh king"? No, we sing "The fight is on." "Am I a devotionalizer of the cross, a follower of the lamb?" No! "Am I a soldier of the cross, a follower of the Lamb."

Look at our heroes. Dr. John Rice was voted out of the Southern Baptist Convention. Oliver Greene was one of the greatest fighters that you would ever meet. Joe Boyd was voted out of the Terrant County Association in Fort Worth, Texas. Dr. Beauchamp Vick was voted out of the Southern Baptist Convention. Spurgeon was voted out of the London Baptist Convention. Lester Roloff was voted out of the Texas Baptist Convention. I was voted out of the Southern Baptist Convention. J. Frank Norris was voted out the Southern Baptist Convention. Dr. Lee Roberson was kicked out of the Hamilton County Baptist Association. Every one of these guys were fighters. They got kicked out because they stood up, and they fought for the Book. They fought for the church, and they fought for right.

I do not care who you are. You are not worth shooting if you are not a fighter. As the song says,

Am I a soldier of the cross,
A follow'r of the Lamb?
And shall I fear to own His cause,
Or blush to speak His name?

CONTEND FOR THE FAITH

Must I be carried to the skies
On flow'ry beds of ease,
While others fought to win the prize,
And sailed thro' bloody seas?

Sure I must fight, if I would reign;
Increase my courage, Lord;
I'll bear the toil, endure the pain,
Supported by Thy Word.

I am going to make a statement you may not like. If you are a man of God that has been called to preach and are not a fighter, you are a disgrace to your calling. If you are a child of God and you are not a fighter, you are a disgrace to the calling of God Almighty.

Now the question comes, what am I supposed to fight? Jude 3 answers that question. "Contend for the faith!" Now, the faith—that is the secret. I am supposed to fight for the faith. I have got to figure out what the faith is. The Bible talks often about *the faith*. In II Timothy 4:7, Paul says, *I have kept the faith.* In I Timothy 4:1, we are told *...some shall depart from the faith.* In I Timothy 5:8, it says of those who do not provide for their house that *...He hath denied the faith.* In Titus 1:4, it talks about *the common faith.* In Philippians 1:27, Paul's desire was to see them *striving together for the faith...* In Hebrews 12:2, *...the author and finisher of our faith.* What is *the faith*? *The faith* is whatever it took to get me saved. That is what *the faith* is. Now, it took six things for me to get saved. Follow me carefully.

I knelt as a little boy in 1937 at the back of the Fernwood Baptist Church in Dallas, Texas, which is in the southwest ghettos of Dallas. I knelt, looked up, and said, "Dear God, if You'll take a little barefooted boy like me, whose dad is the neighborhood drunk, I'll take you as my Saviour." As the song says,

> Oh, happy day that fixed my choice
> On Thee, my Saviour and my God!
> Well may this glowing heart rejoice,
> And tell its raptures all abroad.
>
> He taught me how to watch and pray,
> And live rejoicing ev'ry day;
> Happy day, happy day,
> When Jesus washed my sins away!

FIGHT FOR DOCTRINE

Now, what did it take for that little eleven-year-old boy to be born again. Whatever it took was *the faith*, and I am supposed to fight for *the faith*. Now, the first thing it took was a message. For that little boy to get saved, somebody had to preserve a message. That means that way back before I was ever born, somebody had to contend to keep that message alive. If somebody had not fought for the message, I could not have heard the Gospel. If you do not fight for *the faith* so that little boys in the future can get the same message of salvation, you are not worth the powder it would take to blow you up. I am saying somebody has got to fight. If somebody had not fought, shed their blood, and been martyrs at the stake, I would not have had the message of God.

FIGHT FOR THE MESSAGE

Now, what is that message? First, that message is the virgin birth. I am to fight for the virgin birth. That means when someone says, "I do not believe in the virgin birth," I am going to roll up my sleeves, get angry, and fight. I want to kick him in the shins, knee him in the groin, gouge him in the eye, and fight. You may say, "You've got a bad spirit." I worked for fifty years to get this spirit, and I aim to keep it. By the way, if you do not have a bad spirit about somebody who calls your Saviour an illegitimate child, there is something wrong with you. I will be seventy years old next September. That is why, for the fifty years that I have been a Gospel preacher, I have not one time sat down at a ministerial association with somebody who said that my Saviour is an illegitimate child of a whoremonger who had an affair with a blonde German soldier. I am supposed to fight for the virgin birth.

What are other parts of this message for which I am to fight? I am to fight for the sinless life of Christ. I am to fight for the vicarious death. I am to fight for the bodily resurrection. I am to fight for the ascension of the High Priest Who put His Own blood on the mercy seat.

When John MacArthur says that the blood of Jesus is at the foot of the cross, I want to roll up my sleeves and say, "Shut up, John." Some people might say, "Brother Hyles, you have a bad spirit." I do not have near as "stinking" a spirit as the guy does who denies the blood of Jesus on the mercy seat in Heaven. I am saying that I am supposed to *contend for the faith*. If somebody had not fought, I would not have known about the virgin birth or Christ's sinless life. I would not have known about the vicarious death or the bodily resurrection. I would not have known about the ascension into Heaven. I would not have known the blood of Jesus Christ is on Heaven's mercy seat.

Somebody fought for *the faith*. You are looking at a guy who for fifty years has fought to preserve *the faith* that my forefathers fought to preserve for me so little boys everywhere can get saved and have the Gospel of Christ. I am saying that I am *to contend*. I am to fight. I am to kick, knee, and gouge in the eye for *the faith*.

I am tired of preachers standing up and being nothing more than a glorified, sanctified babysitter for a bunch of baby Christians. We need preachers like the song says,

Rouse, then, soldiers, rally round the banner,
Ready, steady, pass the word along;
Onward, forward, shout aloud Hosanna!
Christ is Captain of the mighty throng.

FIGHT FOR THE PLAN

What is *the faith? The faith* is whatever it took for that little ghetto-bound barefoot boy to get saved. Part of the faith is not only a message but also the plan. I am to fight for that plan. What is the plan? I am a sinner, and all men are sinners. Sinners are condemned to go to Hell. That means when a fellow does not believe that Hell has fire, I am supposed to fight about that. When Billy Graham gets on a nationwide radio broadcast and says that he does not know that Hell has fire, I want to get an old King James Bible and turn to Revelation 20:15 and show him that Hell does have fire. You might say, "I don't believe in criticizing Billy Graham." Then do not ever do it, but keep your opinions to yourself about what I preach.If somebody says that you get saved because of trusting Jesus as Lord of your life, I am going to fight about that. I am going to fight for anything other than the pure simple salvation by grace through faith in the finished work of Christ plus nothing. Earnestly contend for the faith!

FIGHT FOR THE CHURCH

What is the faith? It is a message I had to have, and somebody had to fight so that I could hear it. Now I have to fight so that others can hear it. Somebody had to fight so that the message could be preserved. I will fight to preserve it for others. Somebody had to fight for the plan to be preserved, and I will fight so others can hear it. Bless God, when the next generation comes along, they will not look back and say, "Ol' Hyles trimmed his message." They will say, "He fought for the message and for the plan. He fought for the virgin birth, for the sinless life, and for the faith once for all delivered to the saints." What is the faith? It is what it took for me to get saved in August of 1937. It took a message and a plan. It took an institution that is as much a part of the faith as the blood of Jesus.

When Jonas Salk discovered the cure and prevention for polio, it took the hospitals, the clinics, and the nurses to administer that serum. Jonas Salk had discovered the prevention for polio; but unless there is an institution such as a hospital or clinic to distribute it, it would not have been successful. As a matter of fact, God has ordained an institution to carry the message or the plan; and that institution is the local, New Testament, independent, Baptist church.

When somebody says that they believe in the invisible church," I am going to roll my sleeves up and fight. Well, you might say, "My Scofield Bible has a universal church." Your Scofield Bible also says in those notes that before Calvary, people were saved by keeping the law; and after Calvary, they were saved by grace through faith. Mr. Scofield is wrong. Hence, I am to fight for the local church. Fight! Yes, fight! Why? I will tell you why. Our Anabaptist brethren, from whom we descended, gave their lives for the doctrine of the local church. The battle that they fought in their lifetime was the battle of the local church versus the universal church. Bless God, if they fought so that I could have a local church to tell me how to be saved, I am going to fight so you can have a local church to tell you how to be saved.

FIGHT FOR THE BIBLE

I will tell you something else that it took. When I knelt there as a little lad in 1937, it took a message, a plan, and an institution. Fourthly, it took a Book. That Bible that you hold, the King James Bible, is as much a part of the faith as the cross of Calvary. Somebody has got to give us a word-for-word description of it. God has given us a Bible and has preserved that Bible for us. That means that the King James Bible is a part of the faith. I do not care what denomination or what fellowship says otherwise. Brother, you are looking at a man who has given his life to fight for the King James Bible. You may say, "I use the NIV. What's wrong with that?" Using the NIV is just as wrong as using anything that comes out of Hell. Whatever it took to get me saved as a little boy is a part of the faith, and I am supposed to fight for it.

FIGHT FOR THE METHODS

It took a message, a plan, an institution, and a Book. Fifthly, it took methods. There must be some method, and that method is two-fold: the preaching of that Book and personal soul winning. That is a part of the faith. When Mr. MacArthur talks about personal soul winning is not for this age, I roll up my sleeves and expose him for what he is. They make fun of confrontational soulwinning, passing out tracks, knocking on doors, house-to-house witnessing, and preaching on the street. I am supposed to fight for these methods because that is a part of the faith. Brother, if some faithful preacher had not preached that Book to me, I would not have been saved. If some faithful soulwinners had not tried to witness to me, I would not have been saved. We should fight for the plan and the institution that God has established. We should also fight earnestly for the Book and methods of spreading the Gospel.

FIGHT FOR THE POWER
OF THE HOLY SPIRIT

Sixthly, for me to get saved, it took the power of the Holy Spirit. The fullness of the Holy Spirit is nothing more than God giving power for soulwinning to a saint of God who will pay the price. Some charismatics jump up and say that they talk in tongues like a Pat Boone, who plays and runs with whores and harlots in Hollywood, or a Johnny Cash, who has been in the hospital for dope addiction. They get up and talk about talking in tongues as being filled with the Holy Spirit. That is garbage from Hell. Brother, I am going to stand for the truth about the doctrine of the Holy Spirit.

A lady came to our church not long ago when I was preaching like this. She said to her friend who had brought her, "Who is he mad at?" My friend said, "He is not mad. He really has a heart of love." When I heard about it, I made the tiltle of the next Sunday's sermon was "I Am Mad!"

If you do not defend the message of the virgin birth, the sinless life, the vicarious death, the bodily resurrection and the high priesthood of Christ, sinners go to Hell, Jesus paid the price for sinners, by faith you can be saved, the institution of the local New Testament church, the Book (which is the King James Bible), the method of soulwinning, preaching of the Gospel of Christ, and the power of the Holy Spirit, then you do not have love. I do not care how much syrup rolls out of your ears; you do not have love. I do not care how much honey falls out of your mouth; you do not have love. Brother, you do not have love unless you preserve the message of salvation and the faith so that others can hear the message of God and be saved.

You might say, "I am not coming back tomorrow night." I figured that you were not, and I am going to clip your tail feathers while you are here tonight. I am sick of compromise. I am sick of the NIV crowd. I am sick of the American Revised Standard, New King James, New Scofield, and others. Preachers, when God called you to preach and you trotted yourself to some college, you had a King James Bible in your hand. You did not know it was not the only one until some wicked, Godless professor told you there was something else. Let God be true and the professors be liars. That is the faith! You may say, "Are you through?" Yes, with the introduction.

When I came to Hammond thirty-six years and three months ago, the choir wore robes. Now, I do not like robes on choirs. In 1957, I preached at Bob Jones University when Dr. Bob Jones, Sr. was alive. I was supposed to close out the Sunday morning service. Dr. Bob Jones, Jr. said, "What size robe do you wear?" I replied, "What difference does it make?" He said, "Sunday morning you will be preaching in a robe." I said, "Do you want to bet?" He replied, "On Sunday morning, the preacher preaches in a robe." I said, "That tradition can end. I ain't preaching in no robe." He said, "Then you will not preach." I said, "Good. I'll catch a plane on Saturday and go home." I do not like robes. When I went to Hammond, the choir had the prettiest royal blue robes that you ever saw; but wait a minute, I did not fight over it. Choir robes are not a part of the faith. Some of my dearest friends have churches where the choir wears robes. I do not like it, but I am not going to fight over it.

CONTEND FOR THE FAITH

When I went to Hammond, they would not allow a piano to be played on Sunday morning. A pipe organ led the singing, and there was no congregational song leader. I hated it, but I did not fight over it because it is not a part of the faith. Within six months, we had a congregational song leader. I just stuck one up there and said, "Start waving your hands, and see what happens"; but I did not fight over it. Not using a piano in a service is not a part of the faith. Most of our church fights are over things that I am talking about right now. Many preachers ought to be sure that they limit their fighting to fighting for the faith. The Bible did not say contend for the piano. It did not say contend for the choir to not wear robes. It said, *Contend for the faith.*

When I went down the hallway of our church and went into our church library the first week, I saw an American Standard Bible. Pardon me, liberals call them bibles. I saw the RSV. I saw the amplified, petrified, deified, and putrefied. I saw them all there. I reached up and took all the versions out in the garbage and burned them. I sent them to a place of fire because that is where they came from. You may say, "Brother Hyles, why?" I was contending for the faith. That Book, the virgin birth, preaching—they are all considered the faith.

That means when the music committee got up and announced one Sunday morning "Tonight at 7:00 o'clock, we will have the Christmas Cantata." They had not asked me. I got up after she sat down and said, "Tonight at 7:00 o'clock, we will have old-fashioned preaching." She was messing with the faith. That means when John MacArthur says the blood is not on the mercy seat, I am going to fight about that. When he teaches his lordship salvation and lifestyle evangelism, I am going to fight. That is part of the faith.

Bob Jones University does not let their students go to church on Sunday morning, but they have what they call "a

---

44

worship service" on the campus. Brother, campuses do not build churches—churches build campuses. I said it. We did not get struck by lightning. I exposed your golden image. I am saying that I am here in defense of the local, independent Baptist church. I do not know how you are going to sleep tonight, but I will sleep really well.

It means when Charles Stanley gets up and reads his fake Bible on television, I am going to tell my folks not to watch him. You might say "He is a good man." My mother was a good woman but a lousy preacher. In all the years she lived, she never preached a revival for me. When drama takes the place of preaching, cantatas take the place of preaching, soulwinning is out of date, lifestyle evangelism is in popularity, and the old-time soul winning is out, I am going to fight. Way back yonder before there was ever a Jack Hyles (when there was peace in the world), there were some men laying down their lives for everything that I have fought for tonight. The local, New Testament church—men died for that. Those of you who send your students to a school not wanting them to go to a local church on Sunday morning, you are going to face God Almighty for it.

The blood of martyrs was not spilled for the reason that you think it was spilled. In the United States of America, men were martyred because they baptized by immersion. Baptist preachers were drowned in the very baptisteries of the water that they were baptizing their converts by immersion. Anabaptists, our forefathers, were murdered and martyred because they stood for the local church and fought against the invisible church. Since the book of Acts, men have fought for the faith until you came along. That is why Tom Neal is like he is. That is why this old man is like he is; and bless your little pea-picking heart, we do not have the foggiest intention of changing. That is what the Apostle Paul meant when he said, *I have fought a good fight.*

45

CONTEND FOR THE FAITH

That is what Jude meant when he said, *Earnestly contend for the faith*.

For that little eleven-year-old boy to get saved, somebody had to fight for a message, a plan, an institution, a book, a method, and a power. I have been handed that baton. I aim to carry that baton as long as this old body can take me to the pulpit. I aim to hand it down to the young men that follow me. I will say to them, "Here it is fellows. They fought to hand it down to me, and I fought to hand it down to you." I fought for the faith. I did not fight for robed choirs. I did not fight for a piano to be played on Sunday morning. I did not fight because of committees. I fought for the faith. Earnestly contend for the faith!

This is one of the last letters Dr. Hyles wrote to Dr. Neal.

First Baptist Church of Hammond

In Indiana

Five Twenty-Three Sibley Street
P.O. Box 6448

November 15, 2000

Dr. Tom Neal
Berean Baptist Church
4459 Highway 17 South
Orange Park, Florida 32073

My Dear Brother:

I find it difficult to know how to adequately express my gratitude for all
you do for me and all you mean to me. I tried for 22 years to be to Dr. John
Rice what you are to me. Thank you, thank you, thank you for your friendship
and love.

Now where do I start in thanking you? I feel a little bit like the Apostle
felt in the last of John, concerning all you do for me.

I was pleased with the conference, with the number of preachers that attended,
and was very thrilled to see the health of your work. God bless you, my
beloved and dear friend.

Sincerely,

Jack Hyles

Jack Hyles

JH:mb

Jack Hyles, Pastor   Zip Code 46325   219-932-0711

Enjoy these other great books by Berean Publications!

What Great Men Taught Me
by Dr. Jack Hyles

Dr. Jack Hyles on Finances
by Dr. Jack Hyles

The Journey through Heartache
by Dr. Greg Neal

Can I Trust My Bible?
by Dr. Al Lacy

What You Don't Know about Prayer
by Dr. Tom Neal

BEREAN PUBLICATIONS

A Ministry of Berean Baptist Church
4459 US Highway 17
Fleming Island, FL 32003
(904) 264-5333
(904) 264-9185
Email: info@bereanmail.org
www.thebereanbaptistchurch.com